Parts of Us

Thomas Shapcott was born in Ipswich, Queensland, in 1935. He has published fifteen collections of poems, as well as eight novels and over twenty libretti. Translations of his work in book form have been published in Hungary, Romania and the Republic of Macedonia. He was Director of the Literature Board of the Australia Council 1983–90; Executive Director of the National Book Council 1991–97; and the inaugural Professor of Creative Writing at the University of Adelaide 1997–2005. In 1989 he was awarded an Order of Australia for services to literature and in 2000 he won the Patrick White Award. The Arts Queensland Thomas Shapcott Poetry Prize was named in his honour. He lives in Melbourne.

Thomas Shapcott
Parts of Us

for Judith Rodriguez

First published 2010 by University of Queensland Press
PO Box 6042, St Lucia, Queensland 4067 Australia

www.uqp.com.au

Typeset in Garamond 11.5/14pt by Post Pre-press Group, Brisbane
Printed in Australia by McPherson's Printing Group
Photograph by Sabina Hopfer

Cataloguing-in-Publication Data
National Library of Australia
Shapcott, Thomas W
Parts of us
ISBN 9780702237690 (pbk)
ISBN 9780702237898 (pdf)
I. Title.
A821.3

The University of Queensland Press uses papers that are natural, renewable and recyclable products made from wood grown in sustainable forests. The logging and manufacturing processes conform to the environmental regulations of the country of origin.

Contents

3 Adelaide Lunch Sonnets

1 Parts of Us

Parts of Us

1

We are not born with shadows. They are clambering weeds
that crept up on us while we were not looking.
They do not follow us — we follow them
wondering if there are barbs as well as seed-heads.
Shadows take over whole paddocks of our childhood
but that is not to say there is comfort in numbers:
we had to learn to count.

2

The eyes are faulty interpreters. They pretend to know
the language but do not listen to accents
and are too confident for their own good.

3

Stop! But I did not stop:
neither did you. Some things
exist purely for the sake of rhetoric.
Some things simply call attention to themselves
or merely demand attention.
We are not good at obedience.

4

The tongue is a reckless speleologist;
it is quite unaware of confinement
and is perpetually eager to discover Lascaux.

5

The ears are trapdoor spiders
until the bulldozer clears the paddock
and leaves all our cleverness buried in rubble.
Bulldozers are mobile phones before technology
crept into our side pocket.

6

Never ask the nose for solutions.
Solutions are once upon a time
and smell is older than that.
Smell takes more getting used to
than the thought of a stranger's excrement
in the corner of your own living-room
right on the carpet.

7

Laughter has thorns on the underside
but it has green leaves that shine in the dark.

8

You smiled once. I caught it and held it in my hands
even though the wind was blowing in my face.

9

Tears are dry colours pretending to be a rainbow:
they own nothing but you can't tell them that.

10

Did I commit a sigh? Breathing is always dangerous.
It is like a telephone message in a foreign language –
one that you think you once knew.

11

That was not a baby's cry –
it was the electrical impulse surfacing from far underground,
warning the reptile brain of the death of ancestors.

12

Strange how the skin is not party to the brain's confidences.
It tells its own story and is never truthful.
But what is truth? All things are relative
and the brain is the least reliable of witnesses.

13

To ask questions is to act interrogator.
The witness box has many exits
and witnesses for the prosecution
are not always going to get the colour right –
that is, if there really is a colour.

14

The location of God is in the navel.
The umbilical cord has been severed.
We are on our own.

15

Bones wait. It is not that they have any patience
with calendars. They remember too much, they hoard things,
and when all is said they know there is no last word.

16
Hair tells us we once loved.
Hair is almost impossible to manage
and yet it manages us most of the time.
Hair is the underside of a cloud's imagination
but, caught in the mouth, it brings us down to earth
like a shower sink-hole after shampoo.

17
Did I say we are born without shadows?
And you believed me?

18
The word 'dance' is on my lips.
but dance involves music,
as if music can be notated.
Notation is the mark of our failure.
It is our mark.

Weeding

I have been weeding. My yard is occupied by the enemy
and I am determined to settle this once and for all
though I am perfectly aware that each weed has one
    hundred seeds
and the artillery is lined up against me, simply waiting its
    time.
The earth has always been a battleground, and the air
above the earth is part of the field of action.
Aerial battles were only a logical progression
from musket or sword or elemental club.
I abandoned poison decades back – things have a habit
of sabotaging all our bright ideas one way or another
and science is like dishwater gurgling into the sink –
it seems efficient in the short term but ends up
as detergent percolating in foam down somewhere out of view
yet there all right and set to turn up like a bad penny
later on, when we have spoiled ourselves with all the short-
    term benefits.

We've had rain, so I attack the weeds with proper gusto.
Amazing, though, what the old garden bed lets me unearth:
old bits of plastic, of course; some broken bones nearly
    dirt-coloured,
and is this part of a lock, filled in with compost, and rusted
    to glory?
'Everything is begot by the earth, and to earth everything
    will return.'
Milosz knew nothing about my garden and was thinking
    transcendental things

rooted in common soil, but he was right — no need to think
of the rise of Hitler, or the convictions of Stalin,
or even yesterday's space-shuttle (returned to earth);
we are not worms ingesting rot to make things new again
but we do engage in a type of warfare, and it is true
when I return inside I take a certain pleasure
turning on the tap and scrubbing the dirt off my hands
and seeing how the water takes it all away, and the soap
bubbles, and does the right thing to make my fingers clean
    again
and in the garden outside the weeds are batched in green
    plastic bags
as if the job had been done. Wait, says the earth,
and we all wait. Nothing stays motionless forever.

To Music

Only the young can wholeheartedly love ancient music.
It's fancy-dress, sound pared to its bones
as if the naughty flesh were simply the prop
for the idea of fabulous costumes, or sackcloth and ashes
such as we never dream of today.
                                        Knives flash
among brocades or muskets make rude noises;
perhaps even peasants thump out obvious rhythms –
it's all predictable but safely contained
in our superior sense of what might be.
We live in a world of synthetic synthesised sound,
all blurred into our ears as if we had some say in it,
the manipulators nod and we are nodding too –
it's no surprise but it's not much enterprise either.

This is an era where whole schools of thought
reclaim the past, believing authenticity can be attained.
Music pretends along with the best, and skill
becomes the bright mantra. Let the others sink
in their passive reception of what they are told
to follow, authentic manual performance has its appeal.

I listen to the young performers intent at their task
of purifying the old music with 'authentic' decoration.
The young believe everything. I remember at that age
deploring the habit my father had at the piano,
turning every chord into an arpeggio.

The CD of Mahler playing, transcribed from an old piano
    roll,
reveals the same habit of spreading chords into arpeggios.
There was blood on the old knives, those muskets
were once state of the art — we love nothing perfectly.

Stravinsky in Melbourne

He was taken, with Robert Craft in tow,
to the lyrebirds in a National Park
up in the Dandenongs.
One imagines the car trip
through those endless Eastern suburbs
with stop signs and continuous bitumen
until they finally reached the forest
full of tree ferns and immensely tall trunks
where the mountain ash craned your neck
and positioned us properly.
Robert Craft made caustic notes
and the old man prepared himself to listen.
No bird calls, or at least not the right ones.
They returned to their hotel
and the opportunity was lost.
One cannot imagine lyrebirds,
even the most virtuosic, repeating *Le Sacre du Printemps*
or even *Le Chant du Rossignol*.
But Stravinsky did not come with music
or even much curiosity. Robert Craft
got it right. The composer was tired.
There was nothing more to say.
His last music came out of him like dried pellets.
Lyrebirds have imitated the sound of a car motor
but not, perhaps, the small sigh of indifference.

Vivaldi in Vienna

1

Currency is a charge upon grey heads.
I still have a mop of hair
but not even a wigmaker is interested –
though when it was red
heads turned.
I must forget the past,
it is not negotiable,
but its clattterings imitate my repetitions
as if music had just been discovered.

2

Venice knew me too well:
it knew everyone too well,
that is the cost of a small city
where eyes are trained young
to spy – information is golden
even if canal waters
muffle so much.

3

I must forget old glories –
all those operas are so much sediment
at the bottom of one of the lesser canals –
if I can sell a sonata or two here
I shall be grateful.
More than grateful: I shall eat something.
How many slices of bread
can you translate from one sheet of paper?

I was once spendthrift
with paper as with notes on a page.
Is it possible to starve
on the debris of music?

4

Someone threw an apple core
on the cobbles. You picked it up
for me. Would I have reached so far down?
I wish I could say Yes
but I did not even thank you
for the gift.

5

He was full of himself, that young man.
And confidence is a negotiable instrument.
The principle of double-entry bookkeeping
balances us all out. For every credit
there is a debit. Confidence
feeds on itself as much as on others.
He amassed a cornucopia of musical notes
but the liability was always implicit.
I murdered him out of that confidence
assuming the letters of credit
were as intangible as music.

6

In Vienna a name has no currency,
only the right connection has value.
But I think I am too old for that.
It's not that I am set in my ways;
I am set on

by indifference
by the easy smiles of the young
by the ravages of hunger
when I no longer have appetite.

      7
The cold wind almost ignores me.
Once, I would have called that my victory.

Schoenberg in Melbourne

What if Arnold Schoenberg had taken that job
in Melbourne in the 1930s? He applied.
Imagine the consternation all round –
it would be worse than Nellie Melba supporting
the rival Conservatorium. Imagine *Pierrot lunaire*
being rehearsed in Carlton! Even the Opus 11
would make hackles rise – both were composed
decades previously. But you can't translate
Viennese knowingness to Swanston Street.
Even Freud, in the '30s, was unknown territory
and besides, Schoenberg was Jewish. Even today
he would not be admitted to the Melbourne Club.

But Schoenberg himself? He was used to derision
though he could surround himself with acolytes
and the premise that art was meaningful.
I see it as a sort of death, such a severance
from all he was acquainted with.

Some said he was a pioneer, taking music into lands
without key or compromise, but he had worked out his
        system
and systems, like fugues, belong inside,
not where the sun burns and frizzles and dries out enterprise
turning best plans to, at most, endurance. Schoenberg, back
        then,
might have reconsidered his options. Would he have listened?
People with systems seldom have much flexibility
and Melbourne had inflexibilities of its own to contend with.

The times were not yet opportune. We are a timid people
    and though
a few artists had managed to suck in some sustenance
by getting up early and discovering the lyricism of light
or the way colour and shape unfold in a unique tonal range,
that was only fitfully and in accordance with quite
    derivative expectations.

Rumbles of European angst were beginning to be heard
and the Great Depression had made Melbourne familiar
    enough
with panic and desperation – but music was now
merely the servant and comfort to illusion; it baulked
at the presentation of all the new uncertainties
and even more at the new certainties. Schoenberg was an icon
but he would have come to a place where icons
like the Melbourne Cup or Donald Bradman were secure
as certainties of their own. I think of Schoenberg
as an octopus out of water in this place at that time.

The irony is he ended up in Hollywood.
There, he wrote his Variations For Band
in the old tonal style. Max Reger might have been pleased.

                    A curious postscript
is that in 1949, for his seventy-fifth birthday,
Franz Holford's new Australian journal *Canon* published
his last major work, The Fantasy for Violin and Piano.

By the 1960s
all the young composers everywhere, including Australia,
were aping his tone-row system. Vienna had purged all the
    Jews
but it would be decades before his kind of music
would be declared officially dated.

Perhaps if Schoenberg had come to Melbourne
he might have found a different path to take,
as difficult, perhaps, but with the hard sunlight of an
    Australian
sunshine setting free the old disciplines
and the impossible restrictions.

Monteverdi at 74

1

I have seen too much.
The politics of power,
the access to greed,
even in the supposed humble.
Nero is never a stranger:
he is one of us.

2

I do not have to look far
to see corruption.
Corruption is not a word
to be used about strangers.
It is in our blood,
and the longer we have
the more it resembles
that other word: hypocrisy.

3

I, too, was once young.
I was in love
and my wife died
too soon after marriage.
Feeling is all we have
to cling on to.
Strange that feeling
can be the force
behind corruption,
the guiding power
within hypocrisy.

4

Without feeling
we are automatons
and there are many
who have perfected the art,
which they call 'disinterest'
(not to be confused
with the lack of same).
But feeling will not be denied,
even though it adopts
perhaps strange forms.

5

Love is a strange form.
For me it was a salvation,
a guiding light
through the labyrinth
of youth and the insatiable body.
Interesting that in old age
such feeling remains.
It is perhaps a wonder
even though all the elements
will conspire against us.

6

Corruption is not so much
an absence of restraint
as a surplus of feeling's insatiability.
Had my wife lived
I might have found other forms
to translate this surplus of feeling.
I might have corrupted

myself and others.
As it was, I descended to song
as if that might relieve me
of grief, of tension.
By finding a cadence for feeling
I held time at bay; yes, that is true.
But I also courted pretence –
I could tell that in every listener
who became moved by my music.
No, it was not hypocrisy –
it perhaps flirted with corruption
but it truly expressed me,
or the me I needed others
to respond to.

7

Hence Nero and Poppea.
Do not be fooled
by the wisdom of Seneca.
I am the nurse who rubs hands
at the immediate power.
Nothing lasts
but feeling is not about that.
Welcome to my new opera.
We are all in it,
every one of us.
You will be strangely moved
by the power of corruption.
Is this all we, finally, have?

A Latter-day Polonius

1

Do not look strangers in the eye,
especially in the street. They may
take you up on it,
whatever it is.
This applies in cities,
but country towns have been known
to harbour aggression
as well as defensiveness.

2

Always look your boss in the eye
and any police officer.
There are times when candour
is negotiable.

3

In the eye of the beholder
is your best aim.
Think on it. To act
is to take certain risks
even though nothing is certain.
Not to act
is to remain in the shadow.
No one has honest eyes there.

4

In some cultures
you keep your eyes lowered.
Do you want to be servile
or do you want to be understood?
I recommend
you step as firmly as possible
out of the shadows.

5

I see you but do you see me?
Body language ends at the eyes –
there is all that vocabulary in between.
Remember that the dictionary gets us all
and every person is his, or her, own thesaurus.
No one is completely obvious.

6

When you smile your eyes almost close.
Why is that? There is much to be learned
from how the eyes manage themselves.
Tears also shut down the eyes.
When you keep your eyes open
you might not be easily betrayed
but you also limit what is possible.
It is not realistic to be always wary
but let your eyes teach you
When to be vulnerable. They are more honest
than you are, and they are not always obedient.

Parable of the Second Stone
For Ian George

This is the parable of the second stone.
It is the story of the third stone
and the fourth, and the others that came after.
It is our story.

It is a story that takes place in a land
where the earth has been covered
and the trees kept in cages or in pots.
It is the story of a man
who as a child thought the world was a box
and that fish came from frozen packages
and did not have scales, they had breadcrumbs.
He believed power came from electricity
and he held all the switches.
This man-child became a child-man
and behold, in his entire life
he thought the world was a box and he lived in that box.

He had not been born in that box
but once inside he could hear his own voice
and it was good and resonant.
Inside his box he got used to declaiming not listening.
His friends said he had the common touch
but they did not mean it kindly. He smiled
like the little boy he once was and, safely in his box,

said: Yes, I have the common touch. I scorn the elites.
He said this not only to the elites who shared his box
but in the boxes that united the country.
It was a country of boxes, little boxes and big boxes.

Who threw the first stone?
In the world of parables nobody knows a thing
and nobody confesses. In the world of boxes
nobody is comfortable with a word like 'confession'.
Nobody apologises. Brazen it out,
says the little voice on the inside of the inside.
Always make sure you are in control of the game.
Our child-man had grown proficient at games
so long as they were played in his own special box
where he had arranged all the rules
and let others do his dirty work.
But nevertheless the first stone had been cast.
The first stone was not the last.
The first implement promised the first murder.

Murder. There, it is out.

Even inside his box, the child-man felt a drum
in his ears and he knew the clever implements in his mind
if not in his hands, which were soft and malleable.
We must defend our own, he cried
and his elites busied themselves with repeating it.
The means justify the end, he told his elites.
Yes yes, they nodded and proposed their own agendas.
Which is the way of all privileged acolytes.

Where did the second stone come from?
Some say it was there in the hand, already.
Some say it was brought into him at night
when nobody was looking.
Some say that his box had always been well armed
with stones only they were not called missiles,
They were termed Acts and Laws and Legislation.
Some say ancestral memory is the answer.
It is a force more elemental than reason
and that it has often been orchestrated
by those in command, by those in power.
Power.
There we have the word again,
and it does not mean tame electricity.
It has a tang and a flavour like dried blood
or like meat torn from the flesh of animals.

In his box our child-man kept to himself
but he watched the tame elites with their own agendas
and he realised he had the power
to keep them in their corners
like a lion tamer with his dangerous animals.
It was not a whip in his hand.
It was the second stone.

When did he use it, that second stone?
Already our memories blur, the reports are confusion.
Some say he wanted to join the small band
of Crusaders but they had weapons of mass destruction
and he had only a stone, though that was purposeful
and everyone agreed it has symbolic value.

In the parable of the second stone
there is only one conclusion:
there is never a simple target.
There is never a single target.
Once thrown, the energies are released
and the destruction that follows
will never be exactly what was contemplated.

I do not apologise. I never apologise,
our child-man once said
but that does not mean
the consequences can be avoided,
it does not mean that life outside the box
is not worth considering. The resonance inside
is seduction, but seduction itself has many consequences.

God, the earth, ourselves: we are all witnesses
and participants, and we are all involved
somehow in all the consequences.
The earth has had many terrible woundings
before mankind began to learn respect.
God has been many times vilified,
especially by some who do appalling things in His name.
Ourselves, we crowd out of our boxes
Into the open air and are naked and afraid.

Some of us, sometimes, will find the strength
to be humble, and to learn to be at one with each other.

2 Bound to It All

Bound to It All: Sonnets

MY FATHER'S FEET

Pallid, I used to think: pale and hairless
so that when he wore slippers at night I shut my eyes
and imagined the thick white slugs of his toes
or perhaps the nails, discoloured and featureless,
but reminders of the old Devil in all of us
and as such, utterly obscene. No use
pretending with his judicial pipe and his accountant's eyes:
our dad was mortal flesh beneath that formal dress.

Sons have no pity. I squirmed at night to observe
his unexpected and disgraceful vulnerability.
My own legs were firm, hairy and comfortably free
and my feet gripped the racing stand at the town baths
firmly. Predictable that in the end I suppose
my father's defenceless pallor would fit in my own shoes.

STORM WEATHER

Weather happens. We were fishing, out on the bay
when the first signs appeared. Clouds banking in the west,
all that. This morning ants were among the first
things on the kitchen bench and who is to say
what the chooks were doing downstairs and whether they
had taken the high perch. We always fail the test
of symbols, and let's face it, we had to make the most
of the weekend. The water was blue and sparkling. All
    seemed okay.

We weren't to know how suddenly the change would come.
The fishing had been good, and lunch had been a ball
out on the boat and we did not remark at all
on the sudden drop in the breeze or how the light grew
    dim.
The bay's a big place and dangerous if you're not prepared.
The language was clear. Weather happens and must be
    understood.

SUBURBAN AUTUMN

The Manchurian pears begin their bruised look
from the top leaves down. Soon the Council truck
will start its regular cleanup. With any luck
the suburb will seem spotless though it may take
more than mechanical diligence to work
any real change. It's just as well you took
note of the Green Garbage Day. For the sake
of peace and comfort I'll put out the stack
of bottles and tidy up the front lawn.
Done. No one can possibly complain
of civic duty. Now we can take our turn
at pecking out the eyes and convention
of neighbours. Once I had a backyard incinerator.
I could burn to black smoke all my rancour.

EATING DRIED FRUIT

Papaya – the name remains exotic, and the colour
(red, think of rubies) makes the backyard papaw
of my youth seem the subtropical neighbour
we all took for granted. Papaya brings a splendour
to the equation. But the taste in my mouth has to enter
slowly. This thing is tough! Saliva will labour
with teeth to soften the pellet and uncover
the mystery, which is always recognition, or detour
into self-reference. I think of dried apricots and my
daughter still leads me. I remember, once, dried
watermelon. Tashkent
combining with summer childhoods. I have spent
decades of taste as if that were the solution. All words
are merely the mapmaking in our search. But for papaya,
    the taste,
when uncovered, tells me previous associations will be lost.

WORDS

Words don't last long, or if they do they change.
What I said last week I do not mean today
or if I do, I must alter the way I say
everything, or else you will have forgotten the sense
of it, or I will have. No use protesting, since
language was meant to be like that, a way
of communicating in the dark; once the play
of light was withdrawn there was only sound to convince.

Words on a page are no more than a music score,
notation like cages, but the beast has galloped away —
look at its sturdy flanks — who is to say
what its breath was like, or what the urge in its very core
might have been — we are left with a better knowledge of
        dark
and the mockery of our own breath, with each brief mark.

CHARLES BABBAGE
INVENTOR OF THE FIRST COMPUTER

The mechanical encoding of numbers demands machinery
which doesn't exist but that is not the point.
Nothing exists until it is willed or the means bent
To make it so. Babbage considers every
possibility in his imagination, to foresee each tiny
logic of the mind as cogs in a production plant
or agent in the greater mathematic. He can't
conceive of number other than perfect synchronicity.

My computer has broken down. It's gone awry
or some virus has invaded the perfect logic
of its machinery. Babbage could get frantic
when others queried the ultimate utility
of his 'Analytical Agent' but didn't see
how mind always undermines each great discovery.

MIRANDA AT TWO

My granddaughter is tumbling toward speech.
She can't get words out soon enough. Sound
is the conduit for all those urgent things inside
that must be got out – gesture is not rich
enough. She is already learning much, much
more than scream or tantrum. I understand
this impatience. As soon as she has learned
nuance it is astonishing how ambitious is her reach.

As she stumbles and repeats whole words in a rush
my own tongue thickens and the muscles distort
language so that I hesitate to express myself and cannot
control articulation. Silence rather than speech
is my new mode. Miranda laughs up at me
and says my name with perfect symmetry.

CICADAS

Cicadas outside. How fragile is our security.
I think of the Canadian lakes without frogs.
I remember Christmas Beetles this time of year.
The humidity at night is right. Memory
pulls at the strings, but the beetles do not come.
All these years underground, learning their process:
are the cicadas going to continue their cycle?
We have come to expect the inevitable silence.

You said, do we have anything to talk about
any more? I held my tongue, conscious
of the way speech requires exertion from the mouth
taken for granted until it is no longer automatic.
If we find the cicada shells outside, stuck
to some convenient bush or rail, will we rejoice?

Once I caught the final Moosonee Express
in Canada. We travelled north through sub-arctic wastes
where a fire in 1928 still left blackened husks
of jack pines. Things just do not regenerate.

Today you drove me up to Pine Lake –
it is part of the world heritage wilderness
and the stunted pines there have an endangered look.
This is the bushfire season. We picnic
on the carefully prepared benches where you led me
(my walking-stick was unsteady) along the boardwalk
to this place. The pines looked over our shoulders;
some of them were dying. The kids raced ahead
and their calls sounded like sharp birds
out of sight. Regeneration is no longer an option.

LEGACY

The individual death has its own emergency
but it is nothing. Life has been borrowed,
now it is returned. It is the death
that casts its inheritance on our heirs
which concerns me. Perhaps I am romantic
to imagine some cost or some desolation
or do I seek that? Desolation.
Already the thought has me scurrying
away from myself onto the possessions
they have to allocate. Things tender to me
are not negotiable, even when presented
in song. The bones, the ashes, nothing clings
as much as our own apprehension. Let go.
Easier said. Debt comes unmistakably through.

Four Transformations

1

Rose cuttings are hell, particularly if the rose is old
and the branch is not only thorny but thick.

I have to sit down to attempt this task
putting the cut pieces into a white plastic bag

so I can totter with it, full, to the garbage bin.
It is the weekly collection tonight.

This is one of the few garden jobs I can do
now. This particular rose is ancient

but the fresh thorns are as pointed as the old ones
and new shoots persist. You'd think they'd take the hint

after all this time. Never. The flowers
are sparse enough, though. It is as if

the energy persists in making leaves and branches
but as for anything else, that is another story.

What is my part in this? We are old enemies.
These few flowers persist only because they are up too high.

2

This is the fourth time today I've had a piss.
as soon as I take a drink — water or coffee —

I find myself trotting off to the bathroom
and don't mention dripping taps

I'm like a two-year-old being toilet trained
and yet it is usually only once in the night

my bladder gives the usual warning
and I am all obedience (even in midwinter).

At my age it has to be the power of suggestion
rather than the prostate. (I've had all the tests

including the ignoble finger). The body
has me under control. I could say 'under thumb'

and in some ways I always was obedient.
Who's giving the orders here? Yessir,

whatever you say, sir. Yet, if I go out
I often last all day without discomfort.

I tell myself there's a victory in that,
but not too loud. I don't want to be caught short.

3

Grandpa always sat in his chair in the corner.
He listened to parliament on the radio and smoked his
        pipe.

Grandma was busy. The kitchen, of course, and the garden
but often as not she was off into town

done up to the nines and with lists and agendas.
She was younger than Grandpa. That was the explanation.

When he was younger Grandpa had fine ambitions.
He was a staunch unionist. The world had to change.

Nothing would happen if you just sat down on your arse.
Well, the Great Depression happened, and that was the end
    of that.

I suppose it is easy to say he was a broken man.
We clambered on his knees and asked for stories.

Grandpa spoke of bushrangers and horse-drawn coaches
and the days when Cobb & Co were modern transport.

We listened. For us, it was Once Upon A Time.
For Grandpa it was close enough to hold onto.

When Grandma came back from town we trailed after her,
hoping for treats. It was nearly time for Parliament on the
    radio.

        4
I am a slave to my computer, the little darling,
and am always on the internet. E-mail

is a gift of God or those nerds in Silicon Valley –
Whoever, it is better than the telephone

(especially since my speech has deteriorated)
and I still remember telegrams, hand delivered

and inclined to be serious. E-mail chat
across continents has taken the mickey out of all that.

Dad was a Signaller in World War One.
Morse code and flag signals were things we did in Scouts.

We once had an Aboriginal message-stick
but I don't know where that's got to.

Smoke signals. The cooee (remember that?).
There is a desperate need to communicate.

I only hope the electricity doesn't give up the ghost
though of course there are batteries aren't there?

If I am still around in a decade or so
everything will probably have to be updated.

A pity about the body but, hey,
the age of plastics has probably just begun.

Nocturne

1

Listen. The night is dark
though it's amazing how much light
pretends otherwise – the stars
could be hidden by clouds but this
street and advertisement message
hoodwinks us into believing
our fate is otherwise.
We are alone.

2

There is no silence.
Night engages with a full choir
of possibilities. This emphasises
our solitude.

3

The busyness of light all around us
cannot postpone the eventual darkness that must be.
The occurrence of sound
stitches us into the solitude
of togetherness.

4

So it must be. I do not plan clouds
to obliterate the stars but anyone can see
night is the order of the day – to put it cynically.
Listen to all the musics of the spheres
grinding and dreaming of collision, and I know
the ultimate of silence but I cannot believe
silence truly will happen to me.

5

Night proposes the supremacy of the sun.
The earth, even the earth, believes in the worth of compost.
There is music in that.

Growing Old Ungraciously

THE OLD ITCH

When I was sixteen dermatitis rubbed
my ankles until clear plasma oozed out.
At night I rubbed constantly. My brothers thought
it was masturbation but I had a greater need
and nothing could stop me injuring myself. I could
not prevent it. My skin broke. I can never forget
the itch or the exquisite pain. I think it came about
because of my woollen socks. My skin was held
ransom to that tyrannical urge until
we made the connection. The ankle healed.
But now, over half a century later, my heel jolted
against that old spot and the same itch began to uncoil.
Exquisite pain indeed. Some urges do not die –
they hoard a torment that nothing will satisfy.

EXILE

We learned to live in the place of exile. We grew
and we planted. There was nothing else to do.

We sang sometimes, but song was unnatural for us,
it had a way of stimulating things like loss.

We laughed. It is a noise belonging to the young
and that perhaps is where the whole shebang went wrong.

The elderly do not speak of exile. They know too much
and know that exile has an ambiguous touch —

it surges through the corpuscles of the blood,
it came with us out of the primeval mud

and followed like a shadow or else raced ahead
foreshadowing all we might seek or want or need.

Exile from what? you ask. There is that original dream
of a home place. No things are what they seem.

WANT

What does he want? What does he
want? The tone says it all.
The question is rhetorical.

He could answer passionately.
He could answer with a smile
or, as he does, with a simple explanation:
milk, he says. There is no milk.
I want you to bring some milk.

Not all the milk in the world
will answer his want.
Not all the want in the world
will subdue her impatience,
her need not to be obliged,
never to be obliged.

We drown in our need
or we turn it into a desert.

NIGHT FISHING

They should not have pulled out in the dark.
Knowing the bay and its waters
was no excuse. Night
is another, it takes things away
and it measures differently. Light
is only a stratagem, it cups its hand
into your own and reveals the bones.
Never trust light on a night like this:
and don't pretend that dark
is an illusion that only your eyes are tricked by.
They went out on the water as if this boat
contained them, as if the little lamp
at their feet were sufficient courage.
They gaped at the stars. They gasped
at the pull of tides calling out to that moon.
They were not afraid. Only, when they came back
inshore with their meagre catch, why
did they feel the sand under their feet
with such intense relief? There was no danger
surely? And sand is an indifferent partner
to be afforded such honour.
Nevertheless they kept smiling
as if the night fishing was all a success
and as if each one of them
had never felt threatened.

I AM NOT IN THIS POEM

1

I am not in this poem.
The street is empty most hours
suburbia is like that.
Eleven new fences have gone up
since we moved here,
most of them high.
Street plantings also,
so long as nothing gets too tall.
We have been burgled three times.

2

I am sometimes in the street,
walking places,
and it is true, sometimes I pass people
or more usually they pass me.
Deaths are commonplace on TV
but TV is a shadow of ourselves,
only more dramatic.
We prefer clipped verges
or, better, concrete.

3

This poem is not about me.
For 'I' read yourself,
for 'me' read everyone around here
or even half the population of this country
and remember to think global.
That's your mobile, not mine. Answer it.

4

Have you noticed weeds?
Not only are they persistent,
they have muscles like armoured tanks
and they will take anything on.
It is possible to imagine all this
broken up and invaded,
irrespective of shadows and concrete.
Timber rots quickly in this climate
and salt-damp licks all bricks eagerly.
There are hidden trees just waiting
everywhere and they are not all natives.
I am clinging on by my fingernails
and this poem will have none of that.

5

I was once in this suburb —
you might have seen me in the street
or with my green bag in the supermarket
but it was all shadows. Television
is more realistic than we are
and it can be turned off at will.
We try to believe what others tell us
but life is more cynical than that.
Who am I to say
I am not in this poem?

Old Man Singing

I

If I fart it is the music of the spheres
expressed as the descant to the body's theme
which is always movement. Pay no heed to them,
says the mind's guardian, no one hears
all the sounds round about, and besides, there's
plenty to choose from if it's noise you want. Storm
in a teacup, then? More where that came from,
so don't ever apologise. Apology's useless.

The mind's guardian is an old reprobate,
the jailer who passes you things through the bars of your
    cage
but you'd better pay attention. If you enrage
that very same entity you'll never forget
that you are the subject, never the verb. Your fart
is an unconscious tribute. You could say it is all heart.

2

The body's gas will not stay still for long.
Why should it? It is the product of greed
and appetite; it sings its own sound and has no need
for harmony or counterpoint; it graduates among
both waste and nourishment. That is the thing
with gas — it's not that it should be allowed
to go its own way, but it cannot be stored
like air in an old bagpipes. That's you it is using.

Let go. The long slow note of the body's gas
is really an arpeggio. Did you know such music was within?
Music is the conscious relief that you feel when
all things are in balance; it is the idea of ultimate peace.
Well, hardly. Let's put it this way: some things ease
the mind as they ease the body. We learn from this.

      3
Let me fart while I am still alive.
Gases are ruder once the body is dead,
they have forgotten the virtue of silence, they would
be (for a short while) the final music that we have,
as if everything depended on their brave
exhilaration. Not so. The muscles should,
even at this late stage, contribute some shared
execution of the melody. They have nothing to save.

Some say that last sounds from the body are mournful
but there is always a sort of joy in release.
Think of them as the music of the spheres
come home to roost. The body is still useful,
that is the message. *Music is the one thing that is our own.*
How fitting that it echoes us after we're gone.

      4
The body was once home to many sounds
And the singing voice was most marvellous of all.
Who can forget the truly extraordinary thrill
Of the youthful soprano voice, or the cistern tones

Of the basso profondo? Time melts the ends
From all things, even those loved recordings. All fall
Short or fall out of mind. The voice is a small
Instrument; the whole body fulfils its own ends.

Think of the body's orchestra which contains the lot:
melodic instruments always take pride of place
but though we tend to think of everything else
as accompaniment or the inevitable beat
of pulse or timekeeping we should acknowledge the fact
that all ends up as the last fart, without tempo, without
    tact.

3 Adelaide Lunch Sonnets

Adelaide Lunch Sonnets
For Penelope Curtin and Michael Bollen

EATING IN ADELAIDE

I tasted true figs in Adelaide. No figs before that
were worth the name — shrivelled, dry, a sandpaper taste
or the texture of grit. In Rundle Mall I had my first
discovery; in the stalls they sat in squat
piles, purple and green and ready to split
with pith and juice. Soft as flesh they burst
to reveal that secret place where taste is lost
in all the rich darkness of their heart.

After that, the stalls and markets became
cathedrals of ripe fruit: peaches and apricots,
grapes, plums and nectarines. And my nights
were filled with delicacies of taste that swam
into my mind and into my memory and made
new synonyms for the plenitude of Adelaide

Wine came into my life in Adelaide, years
back. In 1968 my second visit (to Writers' Week)
included a champagne lunch at a winery. It took
no time before the Russian poets roared their verse

and balalaikas twanged. The Australians were more terse
but the bubbles soon were in their veins and woke
the hounds of extroversion in us all. I like
to think Barossa wine sparked from our eyes.

But though I purchased several bottles (this
was the intention) it never had the same effect
in Queensland, so I must assume the act
of South Australian sun and summer somehow was

the catalyst. It made me vow I would return
to test the combination. I came back again and again.

A meal on the footpath, with chairs and a fine table:
it seemed a truly brash extravagance back then
but it's surprising how the habit took. No one
these days blinks at the prospect, no one is able
to imagine otherwise in fact. Impossible
to think back to those ancient times of thin
constricted lives with three veg. and the meat overdone.
We take this all for granted. Let us be humble.

I dips me lid to Don Dunstan, who made this happen.
Adelaide woke all Australia to the great delight
of meals al fresco at lunch or on a balmy night.
Once the appetite in us was finally woken
we took it for granted and settled ourselves in,
as if this was the way it had always been.

To take a meal in Adelaide with friends
is to revisit (for me) fond memories
and to make new ones. Whole galleries
are there for the naming and while I have the funds
this is the task (some task!) I set myself. It demands
true dedication, I tell myself, but it also frees
the spirit of enjoyment and it may release
(as well as appetite) the stimulus of jousting minds.

That is the theory. The facts are more mundane —
wine on the table, and a Menu special to each place.
We have a plethora of restaurants from which to choose
and a lunch hour that can stretch far beyond noon.
So why not settle in? Let us enjoy ourselves
as if this meal were the best and the last of our lives.

Pretend this is the Universal Wine Bar. Why pretend?
Each of us is already seated. Tom's serviette
nestles there on his lap. Michael is not
easily discomforted, and Penelope has found
lots to enthuse over or lots to pound.
On the white cloth crumbs already scatter, it will get
pretty far on in the meal before one of us might upset
enough wine from their glass to bring the waiter round.

Calm yourself. This is a splendid lunch. Such things are
    expected.
Universal Wine Bar knows we are predictable. Indeed,
right from the start they've guessed Michael for red,
Tom for the dry white and Penelope for bubbles. Orders are
    selected
in between talk and discussion. Pretend, as I say,
nothing is unexpected. The bubbles rise in the glass and
    glitter away.

THE PUB LUNCH

West Adelaide for the pub meal, you say. I'll go along
with anything and I've been here long enough to know
I know nothing. West Adelaide is out of the way of the
    show
places in Gouger or Rundle. We push through the throng
at the bar, and I note suits and ties, women with long
scarves and attention to detail. They don't look up as we go
past their Laminex tables. Isn't it always so?
You didn't say 'slum it' exactly, but somehow I got it
    wrong.

I think I was fooled by the slouching boys at the bar.
At a second look, they have come in from the office. The
    Menu offers
snags, but it's printed Chimerosti. What offers
for mash? You say Oven Baked Mushrooms. It's far
too ritzy for a beer, despite the Ocker razzamatazz.
I pick up the drinks list. We agree on the pepperjack
    Shiraz.

The central district of Adelaide (thank you, Colonel Light)
hides plenty of pubs and eating places. A fantasy
to try them all, so today we begin in Pultney:
the Astor. The very name drags 1930 into sight
with images of chrome stairways, porthole windows, bright
Art Deco remnants. They are there in the untidy
corners between bar and billiards. Just as, no doubt, some
    1890
remains (fireplace, sash windows) also get the wrong things
    right.

Luncheon. A dozen oysters – let's be expansive – to begin.
They come with both lime and lemon slices, fat as appetite.
'South Australian oysters are always plump,' I say, not quite
sure where these are from, but prepared to put my oar in.
'My friend says that if they are large and white they lack
    flavour,'
you scrunch up your mouth. 'They're spawning. They taste
    like a sewer.'

CHESSERS

Chessers is the old establishment:
central but discreetly out-of-the-way
which is why (why not?) we've come here today
for lunch at a 'gentlemen's table' as Penelope is wont
to say, though Carol and I are here for the event
with no agendas – except, of course, that we may
catch up on the gossip, the past, the rise or decay
of practically everybody: in other words, we're content
with whatever venue Penelope proposes. This
is a luncheon for specialists in dissection: us.
We give the menu hardly a glance, but none of us guess
when decisions are made: we're specific, precise.
Time, as always, sets the agenda. Time is the boss.
We set to with gusto and yes, this is the right place.

LADY OF THE BIRDS

Our lady of the white cockatoos allows them to wreck
the roof, any exposed wires, the loquat tree.
They scrape the neighbourhood with the sudden drill of
     their cry
but she brings them to home. Fondly, she kisses them on
     the beak.
Our lady of the caged magpie with the broken wing
walks out to the back yard with its refuge shelters
and its tumble of safe places and the magpie utters
an instant greeting, cocking its head in arpeggios of song.
Our lady of the tame native ducks calmly moves
with them and they are at home. Kids from the street
know to bring the wounded things here where they can be
     out
of danger. Our lady of the fledgling doves
that fell from the nest carries them all day to rest
for warmth in the cupped protection of her breast.

SUNDAY LUNCH WITH EVA

It is a seafood restaurant so when we scan
the menu Judith orders dolmades. Eva and I
stick with the oysters (though I think she feels it is my
insistence rather than her experience, but she can
make up her own mind, I suggest). I began
this poem with hints of wilfulness. Why
quibble about the oysters, then? Let's try
the main course. Let's tackle it with élan.

I've seen my immediate target: Moreton Bay bugs,
though this is Adelaide, and they've certainly come frozen
        in.
'With chilli sauce,' I insist. Judith has a slight grin,
'You'll swamp their flavour,' she looks at me and shrugs.
Who could believe a simple seafood meal
would bait us so easily with hooks and a flick of the tail.

AT THE SEA

Glenelg is this: sunshine and water glinting
around jetties and piers. The new promenades face
the Marina where yachts are moored like polite schoolboys
from the proper schools. It's a perfect day and we are eating
inside, behind clear glass, and we are getting
a perfect view of the perfectly groomed and uniform rows
of apartments. 'You can tell if they're empty,' Michael says,
'all the pot-plants are green.' We eye each silent landing.

Penelope is wearing her pearls, to capture the same sheen
as the Marina light outside. It's time to select a dish
'apt for the ambience'. Spaghetti Marinara, fish
(though one choice of duck stretches the analogy rather
        thin).
Who suggested this spot? Light ripples around us to jog
glinting water and sunshine. This is Glenelg.

CHINESE ELM, LATE SPRING, NORTH ADELAIDE

This is a tree that looks at you from above.
How does that place you? I feel the waft and weave
of repetition, which should diminish my sense of self.
Instead, it includes me in the drapery of leaf
and shelter. In this hot climate it might be enough
to look out a window – like now – and become half
a tree myself, because this is the time of growth
despite the warnings of every leaf-fall before. We come
    around with
time which is always the future, no matter how the fall
diminished us last season – think of the sticky spill
of leaves, think of the endless mopping up. Think
of how, right here, recycled shade can mark
certain treetops, taken for granted. My sense of self is
    assured
by the turn in the season. Each new leaf urges me to
    applaud.

LENZERHEIDE
For Karl and Frances Cameron-Jackson

A balmy spring evening in January. In Adelaide? No, it's
    true.
Instead of the always anticipated furnace breath
out of the hot inland, tonight we are coddled with
a most benign air. It is Karl's birthday. 'Let's do
a restaurant,' I say. 'The night's on me. I'll take you to
somewhere serious but not opulent. That means you both
must be my guests.' Frances demurs but quails beneath
my firm gaze. 'Please,' I add, 'I owe it to you.'

As part of our little contest I suggest to Karl
he name the venue. He scours around and phones to say
the perfect place is waiting. We lose our way
before we locate the Lenzerheide. This cool
spring air in summer might be a loaded portent
but we take our seats, determined to make this an event.

PAVEMENT LUNCH AT THE BOTANICAL

'Even the house wine from Maclaren Vale
is superb this year,' Stef says, 'And there's a glut.
Time to buy.' We sit on the pavement but,
hey, this is Adelaide and the chic end of town and all
the tables have a festive air. It's autumn. A frail
hint of coolness is all we need to get
appetites sharpened for the meal. A set
price two-course. On a day like this, nothing can fail.

I think of other meals alfresco. Once
by the Danube in Hungary, another time in Greece, and
     then
I remember the European wasps in Slovenia. 'When
this is finished, I think another bottle,' Michael says with a
     glance
at the waitress, who offers grilled peaches with ice cream.
Today, everything sounds marvellous. You dream, Tom, you
     dream.

There is no season
for ripe fruit, only flavour —
sun bright in your eyes.

Think of mandarins.
Already the stalls are piled
with pillows of fruit.

The peach has no home
except in the eager mouth
longing to taste it.

Imagine soft figs.
Imagination is lost
in taste, instantly.

Fruit piles in the stalls.
It is not greed, avarice
beckons us over.

As if we might own
this half kilo of ripe pears
we fumble for cash.

Grapes. We are their slaves.
Stopping here in the plaza
with dreams of their taste.

Grapes draw in the earth
to invent fluids as if
nothing were the same.

Fruits and vegetables –
they take us as beginnings
for the great journey.

To make the journey
let us begin with flavour –
flavour defines us.

Savour is the ghost,
the added complication
to every repast.

'Fruit piled in the stalls
promises nothing except
imagination.'

What we get is taste.
Which is not to say that fruit
are without surprise.

We eat to be free
of seasons, but seasons are
our true chemistry.

Welcome! I offer
you grapes, pears, apples and figs.
Do the names tempt you?

THE GREEK ON HALIFAX

The Greek on Halifax seems all glass.
I think it dreams of Aegean sun and the glint
of water, though this end of town not even a hint
of that sort of thing is likely – except that this
turns out to be the day the Change appears.
Thirteenth of April, and we note how people sprint
to reach the shelter of this restaurant.
First rain of the season. Red wine time. Here's cheers.

Kerryn is fresh from interstate. She has all the news
but as we pick from the tiers of Mezes, friends come in.
This is the place, I realise, to see and be seen.
Hence the glass walls and the crammed tables: this
is the public side of Adelaide. But Penelope
asks, 'What's this about Alan Jones?' We bend toward
    Kerryn eagerly.

A CELEBRATION IN THE TREASURY

The Treasury building, adjacent to the Adelaide Town Hall,
declares from the outside the solidness of stone,
the regularity of approved design. The tone,
if not pure Adelaide, is sedate enough to recall
a Treasury with money. King William Street is full
of these monumental buildings – banks alone
squat to display a wealth of granite and iron,
the polish that befits a Grand Boulevard. What happened
    to them?

Well, the Treasury Restaurant is the modern world. And we
are here for Penelope's birthday. Tim and Tom
and Michael. Bubbles, of course, but Penelope has really
    come
for the talk of the town, and Tim has an inventory
of news and opinions to keep us busy while the waiter hovers
as we sip and enjoy what the occasion offers.

There is room for fifteen small tables. It is intimate
though the ghosts of office files and documents
somehow adhere – perhaps the faultless casements
and the grand height of the ceilings indicate
digestion of statistics not the delicious intake
of lightly blended food. I will commence
with the tuna (singed on the outside to tingle the sense
with purple rawness within). What would you like?

We commandeer two tables and we meditate on choice.
The white Carrara marble fireplace might suggest
a sort of opulence but it also puts to the test
my vision of clerks and nibs and some supervisor's voice
droning out lists of figures to be added up by hand.
When our bill comes, we accept what the computer has
        said.

NOT A LUNCH SONNET

This is a snack in David Jones Food Hall.
Upstairs and outside the rain and wind come in gusts –
in Adelaide the weather colours everything. No one trusts
a morning sun or a western afternoon squall.
Don't look up at the heavens, that is no help at all.
And the evening Weather Report, for all it insists
on maps and patterns, is mainly recorded lists
of the past. Tomorrow is everything. Forecasts usually fail.

Snug and artificial, this place is the dreamed-of haven.
Students with backpacks crowd in beside plump matrons
doing Thai, Sushi, Yiros. Three forms of chicken tempt
    patrons
into hearty excess and I am tempted too, even
though eating was not my intention. I came for the ride.
Soon enough we will all have to venture outside.

WALKING THROUGH PARKLAND AT LAKE TORRENS

Walking through the parkland along Lake Torrens
this morning two black swans, always a pair;
large numbers of teal ducks; a pelican is there
and five seagulls. I cannot count the moor-hens
but let's say they breed here in their dozens.
The water dimples and glistens and in the trees I hear
lorikeets, magpies, peewees and the whirr
in the damp grass of several topknot pigeons.

Idyllic, I think as I walk across the footbridge
to the university. In precisely this spot
A pair of off-duty policemen did a shot
of poofter-bashing. They jumped with righteous outrage
upon a Pommie lecturer. Relentlessly they taunted him
then threw him over the bridge. He could not swim.

BRIDGEWATER MILL

In the Adelaide Hills this is the ultimate.
The tall stone edifice says 'solid', the glassy
walls of the Fireplace Room confide in us a mossy
embankment. Maidenhair fern is intimate,
peeping over our shoulders. Time to order. Let's create
a lunch to remember. The waiter grins. The world might
    be busy
outside but here eating is seriously easy.
Bubbles are on the house, first glass. I surrender.

Seared scallops with crispy fish, green mango and more:
the menu utters its fantasy. Honey glazed Magret duck,
confit and chutney: entrée and mains. I will take
my share of everything and forget that I swore
to be abstemious. In a place like this
I submit to every temptation. Those ferns wish me bliss.

The Queen's Head crouches at the top of Abbott Lane
'the second oldest pub in Adelaide'
and I believe it. More a cottage, it made
little impression the first time I strolled down
this way, or perhaps it looked like some snug in a town
in Devon or Ireland, say. I imagined it inside
crammed with old pewter and rolling vowels that made
nonsense of Aussie twang, high pitched and thin.

You said, 'Let's eat there, it's just up from your flat.'
and so we walked in. Of course, I should have known
redecoration was rampant and the latest design
favoured 'authenticity'. We stared, then, at
framed sepia photographs as we took our seats
and admired the Sydney rock oysters on our plates.

Main course is duck. Duck as never before.
Duck in four dollops in the great white plate.
Duck sausage, duck breast, a pâté in its small white
bowl, and finally neck of duck. Sure
of his authority the waiter instructs the four
diners on the order of eating. 'You must create
the proper sequence. Begin from the right
with the sausage, and then move left from there.'

Tom, being left-handed, had already put his fork
into the knotty neck. He pauses, and takes care
to follow directions. The waiter was right. There
is an aptness to the order of things. Each taste leaves its mark
and every gradation is catered for in this place.
They toast the occasion. Even the wine has grace.

THE URBAN ON FULLARTON ROAD

Adelaide hoards its surprises. Here on the edge
of the South Parklands and predictable suburbia
The Urban seems another motel annexe, familiar
as Laminex. The surprise is in the menu, witty
and succulent, a cross between self-conscious arty
and something out of your own backyard (or similar
safe environment). You get the picture? Theatre
and a sort of matinée good health, everyone's party.

And everyone is here. We crowd past the busy tables
and at first the sudden hubbub drills our ears
but it is surprising how soon, seated across
from each other, the noise no longer nobbles
our own collusive chatter. Each taste is precise
as the spring sunshine, and this is a very clever place.

THE ART GALLERY CAFÉ

Lunch in the Art Gallery Café is the necessary thing.
Today on the terrace there are the three of us:
there's me, there's Rosemary and of course there's Tessa.
Tessa's an old habitué, the waiter will bring
her bowl of water and she will go along
with that, although she's more interested in who's
around – that troop of school kids looks propitious:
now they've seen her and they begin to throng.

We turn to the menu. Something light perhaps?
This is a place of large plates and small serves,
ideal, I think, for when summer's hot and our nerves
are jangled with examination marking. Tess leaps
towards a little girl who softly asks her name.
All children are different, and they are the same.

TREASURY AGAIN

After a string quartet recital in the Town Hall
Janacek rumbling and Dvorak still lilting in our ears –
it seems apt and companionable to walk the few paces
to the Treasury for an after-concert meal.
Dinner is still being served and I'm hungry. We will
have the oysters and a Main, I suggest. No, it's you who says
oysters. I who agree. We raise our glasses
to the musicians. They deserved to have the house full.

Savouring our food (I've never seen oysters stacked
in a pile of shells before, except when torn from the rocks
on a Queensland beach). I have one of those small shocks
when I hear my own name spoken at the next
table. Who would not be surprised? Who would not be all
    ears?
Those people are strangers. We wait till the next clue
    appears.

Kent Town is a name that in itself spells out
a sort of village ancestry, not an inner enclave
with only the parkland before you arrive
at Rundle Street and the Mall and the trendy part
of Adelaide. The Tin Cat is an old cottage that
is a nest of tiny rooms all of which have
Laminex tables, a squeeze of lunch patrons and live
baby noises to ensure we get the mood right.

We squeeze ourselves in. Then, to the waiter's wonder,
'Three dozen oysters,' I say. 'No,' I insist,
'there are three of us and hunger overrides cost.'
The pile of shells mounts on the table's centre
and the family groups around loosen and sprawl.
No one's complaining. Lunch hour envelops us all.

A MELBOURNE LUNCH SONNET

If we do it in Melbourne style, let's make it special.
Grossi Florentino at the top of Bourke Street
is as good as you might get for a luncheon date.
Upstairs, rather than the downstairs à la carte, and with all
the trappings. Antipasto for starters. Not your usual
platter but two separate selections. On each plate
four prepared concoctions blended to re-create
impatience in the taste-buds and readiness for the main
      meal.

We choose. You smile and we each raise our glass.
But the sorbet that comes after, before the cheese,
intrigues with a subtle blend we cannot quite place.
Pear, the waiter explains, with cinnamon as its base.
We nod, of course, but then we both proceed
to tackle the cheeses with something like original greed.

8 HAIKU

Adelaide takes heat
and as if the true centre
were elsewhere, tests it.

This is the place of
extremes. I should mention light
but I think of dark.

Dark is our obverse.
That is not to say that shine
avoids us wholly.

Then there is delight.
We stumble to acknowledge
the craft of sharing.

My share, your share. See
no need to consider taste.
The lines have been drawn.

I consider taste.
I revel in it. I ask
Nothing but its claim.

Do we all come home
to this? Do we share flavour
or can we link taste?

All answers are Yes,
with summer a sky of light
and our glasses full.

FOOD

When I think of Brisbane I think mudcrab.
In Melbourne for some reason I think rack-of-lamb.
Vienna will always be asparagus – I came
There one year at the time of the Spargelfest. I'll dob
in San Francisco for oysters, but then I jab
at an imaginary plate in Port Lincoln and in some
tables of Adelaide: oysters are too hard to name
any ideal place, you make your own stab.

The point is, cities and places tweak the memory
with tastes and flavours as much as sounds and sights.
I think of Doyle's on Watson's Bay on balmy nights
and of yabbies I once ate in the new finery
of the Adelaide Festival Centre. Taste-buds
are as nostalgic as all the pellucid words.

John Olsen once served me preserved olives
in his home at Clarendon a recipe he'd brought from Spain.
When I taste olives these are the ones to haunt me again
in their impossible tang. The taste lives
outside of itself, only a romantic believes
it will ever be recaptured. Now it's your turn
to pin down the moment when a taste spiked its pin
into your memory. Oh yes, taste deceives.

In Moscow, once, I had true caviare. Is that boasting?
I round my mouth longing to catch the flavour
and an austere Prescinkt tight with the chill of winter
is all that hovers. In Adelaide hot sun is beating
outside and it is time for lunch. Have you tried the oysters?
They're not spawning yet. Once tasted, they are relentless
        masters.

As nostalgic as every pellucid word
I sink into all the cities and suburbs of taste.
Food is the same in Florence as Firenze, have I missed
something? Once, by the Arno, I overheard
some Americans complain there was no butter on their
        bread.
Amazing what we carry with us, and at what cost.
I munched my own panino and ham. They tossed
theirs aside. Perhaps all taste is more or less absurd.

Are we always wary encountering something new?
My first night in Ubud I was lured outside
by the languid smells of tropic air, though each dog
in the village accosted me. But in New York I grew
fearful on my first evening out. I laugh now. Why hesitate
when so many rich flavours are heaped upon our plate?

BEQUEST

In my bank I have saved just enough
for a small funeral, although I do not want a funeral,
let the medical students play with all
my remaining parts. I have bits and pieces of stuff
such as you might find in a garage sale, at a rough
guess most of it won't be given away — it will
gather in back rooms and bottom drawers for a while
until my descendants cut the clutter from their life.

What I do have is an eye that sees the mess
of pittosporum petals covering the concrete floor
under the tree until, for a week, the space is a rare
and fragrant carpet. But, unlike a carpet, this
is a gift that can't be measured. I wish my heirs
(if only once) the same gift. And to make it theirs.

4 Still Life

Still Life with Skull
for Don Rankin

A glass half-full of whisky,
that is what sets the mind in motion
first. And it is waiting
for the familiar lips, the caress
of soft flesh to fulfil its purpose.
Behind it, the uncut lemon
hints at all the usual promises,
the expected tartness.

Or perhaps the glass of the flagon
draws attention to itself,
possibly even before the mind takes in
the bizarre spectacle of an opened rose
displaced inside. That must have been
when it was still in bud. One thinks
of ships in bottles, other tricks
playing upon the idea
of narrow openings. The rose,
once seen, adds its own discomfort.

The sheep's skull balances the composition.
That is all. Had it been human
domination would be complete.
Does that mean we do not take animals seriously?
Death, yes. But this is merely impersonal.
The glass of whisky waits. The rose
tells us deliberation is all. We imagine finding

possessiveness and a still-warm breath.
The skull once hid behind lips of a sort,
the sockets held eyes, nerves,
perhaps even tear ducts.

The Haunting
for Gordon Shepherdson

It was just ordinary bush, but this was at night
so things seemed to have moved. Those trees were not there
in this way before, and tussocks became pitfalls,
easy slopes assumed different attitudes
and were almost malign – or was he dreaming that?
He felt he had to be in charge; after all
it was his decision in the first place
to bring her here. He'd known it since 'forever'
like the back of his hand, he would have said,
and on weekdays nobody was ever here,
so an evening camped down by the water
seemed the sort of private getaway
where anything might happen – or nothing at all,
(he realised she had a part to play in this).
But after, they had put the fire out and nothing had
    happened,
though she had given a sort of promise. That was when
    dark
surrounded them suddenly. He realised
the car was way up there, on the dirt road.
They climbed carefully and he put his arm
to shield her, but the darkness came between them
and it was an awful long way to go. Anything could
    happen,
that was even before the noises had begun.

Drought Flowers

They chopped the red-flowering gum
because a branch died
so the messmate tree, its parasite,
grew strong and last year
it covered itself with pale bloom.
Life moves in cycles.
But in this year's January heat
there is a new thickening of leaves
as if the messmate has hosted
its own incubus.
We realise suddenly the original tree
has sent forth vigorous shoots
out of the stump the Council decreed
worthless.
Red flowers, in great bunches,
weigh down their sappy branches
and the bees, like us, rejoice.

Three Pieces

for Katie Noonan

LITTLE BOYS

They have bodies like eels
but they splash in the water
out of water which is where they came from
and that is in a way true
except that there is no water
more wonderful than the water
of their laughter —
that does not come from their throat
it was from somewhere deep inside
a place you recognise
welling up so you catch your breath
as if even that were precious.

LITTLE GIRLS

So much movement is a sort of dance
they can't help it, it springs
out of their limbs as if limbs
were intended for this: rhythm
born before birth, pattern in the design
of each muscle and already reaching
towards agility. Music came later
after rhythm, but put the two together
and you have the perfect accompaniment
for the dance. Didn't you know this?
She tosses her head, but it has already begun,
this letting go so that the contours
of even the youngest body are exploring
what music was for, before we shackled it.

PARENTS

Yes, it is true parents are a loan
but that doesn't tabulate the cost
of parenthood nor the uncomfortable joy
being a donor indicates. Perhaps the thought
was first initiated by children. We are all
embarrassed by debt and to think of our own parents
in this way somehow puts us on the negotiating table
with a certain advantage, debt is a means
of proposing a definite perspective.
But now to be parents ourselves –
suddenly the perspective changes
and the imagery of debt turns in
on itself, as if there were nothing to pay
nothing either party could possibly give
except love, and how compromised
is that already? The self
has become a strange creature; it thrives
on love, but it grows robust on challenge.
Parenthood is a loan, of course,
but who is the debtor, who the receiver
of this bounty?

The Rat

Promise or curse? I suspect the Black Death
Of 1347 got my ancestors onto their North Devon estate.

We might easily call them 'squatters' now.
Times were grim, though the land became theirs.

Well, that farm it now a bed-and-breakfast
And our branch skipped the county generations back.

I was once in a kampong in Malaysia
Trying to sleep on a reed mat. It was a timber floor.

At dawn I got up and made for the washroom outside.
Too late. A visitor was before me.

And already small boys were giggling through peepholes.
A large black rat dived into the hole in the floor.

I decided I could wait. More like an ancestor
Than a stranger, that rat put me in my proper place.

Loss

Is there such a thing as loss? Everything is gain
in some way, surely? The loss of childhood
is an immediate gain in maturity. Most of us
do not regret, unless we are irredeemably sentimental,
those times of being bullied, of being ordered about,
of being surprised and enchanted by small things.
Adolescence, too, is that time of pimples, clumsy
attempts at mimicking your elders, nights of sterile
    dreams.
So, you can write it all off, the past. Or can you?
As you get older you lose so many things that loss
is merely relative. Hello, cousin. No, don't turn around
you'll miss another funeral. What is the gain in that?
The answer sounds like cynicism. And all the while,
like some faulty bank investment, these things mount up
and who is the debtor, then? What is the logical debt?

Sestina

What things do you remember about your dad?
And what things did he hold onto about his father?
And beyond that? Has there always been something to learn?
What things are carried on, what things are abandoned?
We do not start with a blank sheet – our genes
see to that. There is an itch somewhere in the shadows.

Under the house, there among cobwebs and shadows
was the old workbench, the bottles of nails, and dad
making crude children's toys from old wood, his genes
still rapping his knuckles with the rod of his own father
who was a neat craftsman, and never abandoned
one stick if it was re-usable. Dad had much to learn.

He never quite got the knack. Some things we learn
by example, some are inherited. All the shadows
of war came between them – when he abandoned
home comforts for a boy's dream of adventures, dad
did not think of precept, nor of mother and father
betrayed by patriotism. There was bravery in his genes.

He grew up in the succeeding years. Genes
have no part in this. He was set in a context to learn
mud, and mateship, and indiscriminate slaughter. His
     father
and mother remained, at most, insubstantial, shadows
against the realpolitik of warfare. Dad
might have gained early maturity but something was
     abandoned.

I just recall my own grandfather, that stern old man, who
    abandoned
the old England, though it remained tight in his genes.
He stayed with us often, and he bullied my dad
into copying, badly, his craft skills. When will we learn?
The old man still sends orders out from the shadows.
We still hear the undying voice of the father.

It goes back a long way, father into father
as if nothing were gained, nothing abandoned.
I went my own way (we all do) but inheritance shadows
us. That is the unsatisfactory thing about genes.
It does not matter what tricks we learn,
in my own voice I hear the dead cadence of dad.

I pick up the saw, the nail, this hammer. Dad,
you were an indifferent carpenter, but the shadows
fall across me, as they did you. That is to be a father.

What Happened to Love

What happened to love? I remember, and I do not regret,
the pulse of pure ardour that turned night into day,
that provided me with guidance enough to sway
any doubts from my mind and you were the imperious
    thought
that took me there. You were the certain light
conditioning me to the very idea of ecstasy.
So what if I thought you were as one with me –
the best dreams of the mind are always hard to beat.

Well, that was decades ago. The past
simply proves we did not really know – nobody does.
But let me put it this way: the times may pass
to make us cynical but nevertheless we lost
nothing, and we did discover a way
to keep us exploring. Do we need more? Do you agree?

Skin Deep

What if the soul were expressed most honestly by the skin,
not some interior cavity, the cave of consciousness
or the liver of unsatisfied hope? The mess
we leave behind and the plans we will never attain
can be quite easily brought to the foreground, then
laid out cheerfully (or otherwise). The less
we think of ourselves as interior consciences
the more we approach the surface that is our own.

Think of it. With age, the blotches come to the surface,
the thick skin relinquishes itself to make
a pact with mortality. The soul hastens to take
precautions, as is necessary if it is to practise
its basic pact with time. Did you suppose
immortality was the issue? Your skin already knows.

Night Mugging

He wasn't afraid of the dark;
that was years ago, and besides,
his mobile and his ipod were constant –
even on trams and in trains
he could not feel alone
and that was part of it, or used to be.
Darkness, though, has a way
of creeping up on you
and light is only to throw shadows.
He was old enough to know
how to look after himself
but not old enough to save his ipod
or his leather jacket or the Blundstones
he was so proud of. Even in the dark
he stood out. The mobile phone
was only useful to him after the event.
But even that was a matter of confusion –
he kept spitting blood and broken teeth.

Period Portraits

WIDOW

On summer days she was up very early
planting a row of petunias or watering the maidenhair

because in the heat of mid-morning she wilted
and reclined, now, in the living-room chesterfield

though when Arthur was alive she chided him often enough
for retreating with his pipe to that same corner.

She never listens to the radio. He followed parliament
religiously, as if he still had a say in things.

Not so long ago she was the tyrant of the kitchen
but with only herself in the house she does not need to
    bother.

The neighbours, though, still have to envy her garden
and she has always enjoyed a good show of flowers.

Arthur said, once, she must have been born with green
    fingers.
She was born to work. When will it ever stop?

THE SMELL OF COAL-DUST

1

The smell of coal was what he liked best. His dad
came home from the mines usually around 3 o'clock
and had a hot shower to clean the stuff off
(the mine owners did not believe in hot water)
but, coming in from school, Teddy still got the smell
and though his father said 'It's a dog's life, son,'
he knew what he wanted and nothing would stop him
or deflect his ambition. His father died
coughing and protesting, but by then it was too late:
Ted was one of the late shift. When they took round the hat
he thanked the manager and thought of his mum.

2

Things had changed. It was all open-cut now
and efficiency was part of the vocabulary.
When Ted became foreman, then part of the management
    team
he dimly remembered hot showers and his father's stench.
There was no glamour in coal. But once, late at night,
when the old steam train had been dragged out for the
    excursion
Ted caught the old smell, and did not know whether to
    laugh or curse.

GLOVES

'It's the things I can touch,' she said, 'They give their power
to me, and I can make that my own.' She smiled

but she might have well have wept. 'We handle so little,
I used to wonder at my mother wearing gloves

but it's easy for us to forget utterly
that touch was not allowed.' Her fingers were probes

that made her hands seem almost too restless,
if it were not for the calmness in her eyes

which she kept open as if sight might help.
'There are other things that you must learn yourself

if you are to survive. Even as a sweet young thing
I wouldn't come at gloves. My mother was in despair

thinking of neighbours. But I thought only of myself,
and that was wise. It is only through self that we encounter
        others,

as I was to learn.' Her fingers became her eyes,
and her touch became her great communication

but the day she found her mother's abandoned gloves
she held on to them. It was as if the old lady were scolding
        her still.

GENEVIEVE

1

She kept a pet sheep in the back yard. It was once a lamb
and then it was allowed to grow. Nothing would stop it.

Instead of getting her husband to put it out with the other
    sheep
she fed it daintily by hand still. It always came to her

and though she no longer tied a ribbon she mothered it
    still.
And then one night it got out. It had found the rams.

'Oh, but you smell!' she scolded. But it was no use
    pretending,
something had happened, and it was no longer her pet.

Her husband, jokingly, suggested it was ripe for slaughter.
    She did not smile.
After a few weeks it was clear her pet was with young.

Her old hands did not even tremble when she unlocked
    the gate and shooed it into the paddock. She had no
    children of her own.

2

On the enclosed side veranda she always prepared morning
    tea.
Sometimes he joined her. They seldom spoke. 'The weather

is bad this year,' he would say, or, 'that mob in the top
     paddock
are just about ready for the sales.' Sometimes she would
     reply.

The ceremony of the tea did bind them together somehow.
There was something companionable, people usually said

though at night she put off going to bed. He was in early,
dead to the world. It had not always been like this.

                3
At boarding school she was praised for elocution
as well as her piano. She still plays some pieces
     perfunctorily.

Somehow it isn't the same. Beethoven died centuries ago
and who is there to listen, anyhow? Genevieve still
     practises,

it is the only way, and she sees it as a sort of victory
– over the past? Over time? Over all the others that ever
     were?

Somehow the music has become, at most, a sort of cage
and it is years since anyone, including herself, has really
     listened.

That lovely speaking voice, too, has grown dulled from lack
     of practice.
These were not the things her husband prized in her.

He saw her, once, riding across his top paddock
and he knew immediately that she was the only one.

So it goes. She does not speak of disappointment,
nor does he. They both recognise the fact: she was the only
    one.

CLASS ACT

At thirteen he was six foot four. His buck teeth
and cornstalk hair should have made him a clown
or the court jester. He was top of the class.
The form bully sidled up to him. Gilbert took it all
for granted – his popularity, his relaxed smile
and the ready acknowledgment of all the boys.
None of the girls in the class had to make way for him
and he treated everyone as just good mates, which was in
     order.
'He will go far,' was the portent hanging over him
and he could grin at that –it meant nothing to him then
or ever after. He might have been the ugliest boy in class
but hadn't that always been so? Water off a duck's back.
That easy jocularity and the quick mind for words and
     numbers
took him to the first job at hand, selling advertising space
in the weekly free newspaper. Gilbert was well known all
     right
and he would just earn enough so as not to bother.

NEPHEW

His uncle was the engineer – all those famous bridges –
but Jack finished school at thirteen. He was apprenticed
to a good tradesman in the Railway Workshops, which
    meant
his whole life was taken care of, except that now and then
someone reminded him of the illustrious name
until in the end he changed it by Deed Poll.
That didn't help. Old schoolboy acquaintances
had a way of turning up now and then
and they always used his abandoned name
or if they did not they thought of it
And again the old associations festered.
Sometimes he thought he would never be himself.
It was as if some genetic tyranny
must taunt him with a sense of failure,
a sense his uncle could never have understood
or if he had, it was too far in the past
and meant nothing, nothing at all in the end.
His uncle had encountered demons of his own
and a sense of failure that was just as real.

THELMA

Thelma was incorrigible. At thirteen
she had boobs big as her mother's, and only boys
in the upper school would satisfy her. Mr Hoffmann
once forcibly removed her from the classroom. She spat
in his face but rather enjoyed his vehemence
and the muscles of his arms which strained the cotton
of his summer shirt. She kept a lookout and one night
when he had a beer with the boys at the Exeter
after the cricket match she sat in the beergarden
(always so badly lit) with lipstick on and the miniskirt
that humoured her solid but well-proportioned legs.
'I see the town bike sitting outside,' one of his mates said
and it was not Stan Hoffmann who lurched out, later,
and it was not Thelma who went off, disconsolate.
She had made her move. It would not be the last.

Autobiography

I

Modernism was the great period of destruction,
that's why it was so exciting. It still is.

I grew up with modernism tugging my consciousness
but there was also the past I had to discover

or even recover – time slipped out of mind,
at least for the moment, and after all, to get modernism

I had to know what it was reacting from
and even then I knew the best part of its energy

was in its cheeky or insolent reaction.
As a teenager I thought I could understand that

and the journey was full of the best discovery – surprise.
No wonder I shocked the family. All that revolution.

Well, revolution it was. I was taken round and round
and before I got off I was given a constructive stimulus.

But the past is itself a certain aphrodisiac.
I think it first addressed itself to me through music.

The implicit elitism of modernism (those arcane references)
Tilted me firmly into that sense of exploration

which is essential to every developing mind
and it has to be remembered that 'popular' music ('The Top
    Ten')

at that time was the property of Tin Pan Alley.
No one dreamed it was possible to make your own music.

The great and true revolution of the 1960s had not begun
(it has to do with inclusiveness not exclusiveness)

but I leapt across the stubborn barrier of time
and found myself entranced by the community of the
    English madrigal.

Later I came, devotedly, to Bach. Forget the plonk
poured by the gallonful into the ears of my brothers,

I had come home. The *perruques* could not disguise
that immediacy and that inevitable sense of balance.

I also discovered Mahler (This was in the era
of 78 rpm discs, long before Mahler was standard
    repertoire)

so music led me into the past. There was also poetry
and the discovery of my own literature.

I read *Mahoney* at sixteen and never looked back.
Judith Wright, up on Tambourine, showed me poetry
    could be relevant

and that language held off the darkness as much as
    anything.
The where and the when were necessary but secondary;

those moderns I so loved were part of an old story;
they lived in their own time but had something to say to
    me.

Why should I be surprised when I finally came to choose?
The conventions of each age may take some getting used to

but that witty and knowing man, Chaucer, knew a thing or
    two.
I count him as an old friend. Come in; join the party.

    2
Postmodernism was like the sort of joke that is not really
    funny.
It was not meant to be. Irony was the mode

and that depends on a superficial sort of knowingness
certainly far removed from knowledgeability.

That was not an infection in the left eye,
it was the wink that is needed to keep you impressed

or at least in the picture. The trouble with irony
is that it takes itself seriously,

at least while it is telling you it is not serious at all.
('History is dead' and all that rot.)

Postmodernism was all into playing games
But games had a way of turning into competition

and so I was lost to it. I believe in the spirit of play
but that has to do with the concept of joy, of celebration.

You've got it: Postmodernism heavily discounted feeling
as if we were too sophisticated for that. Feeling's universal.

Stravinsky, of course, had prefigured postmodernism back
    in the '20s,
when he abandoned folk inspiration for the artifice of the
    eighteenth century

but by the mid 1930s it all seemed pretty sterile
and *The Card Game* played dangerously with self-parody.

('Look at me looking at myself: there is only one solution
    and it is irony.')
But all around him Europe was rehearsing for the
    Holocaust.

Music is incapable of expressing emotion was one of his sayings
    at the time.
It was part of his repertory of po-faced jokes. He was taken
    seriously.

Only when he moved to America and was beguiled by
    Auden
did he discover in *The Rake's Progress* (Thank you Auden,

or was it Chester Kallman) that music can turn simple card
   games into drama.
The card game in that opera holds us riveted,

we are struck by the plight, and the pathos, of the human
   creature.
Feeling, again. Something is stirred, and it is not the
   necessary artifice.

9/11 marked the effective end of postmodernism.
Its father was probably the arrogance of Western
   imperialism

and its mother was fixated on fast food and flat-screen
   television.
Like the rococo it was indulged for its own sake

and there were some things it did extraordinarily well
but there was something missing. What it gave

it took back and demanded compound interest.
Postmodernism was the accountant, the bureaucrat

And, like Eichmann, or like his lesser follower, Ruddock,
the simple condition of feeling proved too uncomfortable,

it all demanded something; it was that feeling still exists
   among us.
We might be on our own, but we share more than the glint
   of irony.

3

'In the end, there is only your self and my self.'
Wilfred Owen, wrote that, and I remembered

though I did not note at the time, where and how and why.
I have never found that quote again

though it has served me well, especially when I am asked
'Who do you write for? What is your audience?'

The myself is sufficiently there (at least, I hope so)
for individuality to take voice, even in the borrowed spirit

of a common language. And the yourself
is similarly borrowed, unique. I believe in communication

despite the worn material of common words.
Inflection can be contagious, even on the printed page.

Assertion always carries its own question mark
And plea is always another way of inviting others to the
        feast.

We quote from others to assert our own individuality
as well as some more common heritage

or as a display of necessary or unnecessary erudition.
History is in the very sinews of our language.

If I think of you, it is that part of myself that is universal
and unique – which is to say I have learned from others

in the long conversation that has brought us here.
I cannot believe we are alone

not while so many voices resound in my head.
The myself I celebrate is never fully isolated

which makes the yourself a vast company.
To be unique is to remain still a part

of that company. Language ensures this is so,
and to be imperfect is part of the deal.

So I might sit alone in this chair or at my computer
but that has nothing to do with the heart of the matter

which comes back to the erotic wonder of feeling;
as if it were ever otherwise. It is all in the telling.

Solitude

This room is always crowded. Solitude is an ideal
but hardly reasonable. There are echoes everywhere.

You are located in place. Place is never without context
and you have almost wilfully built a nest of associations.

The world is by nature inhabited by others. You are not
    unique.
That is the first lesson and it is hard to learn.

You think that being born was a unique event?
It is the great commonplace. All the others

have gathered around, it is a celebration,
and you are the least important member of the party.

You imagine that dying is the real act of solitude
but crowds have gathered, even in the desert,

as your genes salute all the ancestors
and you have already passed on their imperfections

to the descendants. Even your language
is the common tongue and your final silence

simply rejects that language but it does not abandon it.
This room is far too crowded. When you are not here

that will be the time for the settling of associations.
that will be the time for others to contemplate solitude.

Acknowledgments

Poems in this collection have appeared in the following journals:

> *The Age*, *Antipodes*, *The Australian*, *Australian Literary Review*, *Blast*, *Blue Dog: Australian Poetry*, *The Canberra Times*, *The Griffith Review*, *Heat*, *Island*, *The Mozzie*, *Overland* and *Wet Ink*.

'Parable of the Second Stone' was read by the author at the Anglican Synod in Adelaide in May 2003. 'The Adelaide Lunch Sonnets' were originally published as a limited edition book in 2006.